TAKE CHARGE OF YOUR LIFE!

LANSON ROSS

HARVEST HOUSE PUBLISHERS
Eugene, Oregon 97402

TAKE CHARGE OF YOUR LIFE!

Copyright © 1986 by Harvest House Publishers
Eugene, Oregon 97402

Library of Congress Catalog Card Number 85-081932
ISBN 0-89081-515-1

To my friend Dr. Merv Rosell,
whose Christian character and commitment
I have never doubted.

CONTENTS ———————

I
DECIDING TO CHANGE THROUGH SELF-DISCIPLINE

II
EXPLORING SELF-DISCIPLINE

III

PRESCRIPTION FOR SELF-DISCIPLINE

IV

SELF-DISCIPLINE AS A SOURCE
OF JOY

V

MAINTAINING SELF-DISCIPLINE

I

DECIDING TO CHANGE THROUGH SELF-DISCIPLINE

1

Can I Really Change?

It is often said that you can't teach an old dog new tricks . . . but no one has ever said how old is old.

Is it possible for someone who has battled a habit all his life to change?

Many of us, both young and old, have wished some things were different in our lives. For some it involves weight control. Other people suffer from a violent, seemingly uncontrollable temper. Still others of us know the pain of an entrenched habit that won't let go. The battle appears endless for those of us who struggle with self-discipline.

We have learned from watching others that self-discipline is the fulcrum in the lever of action. Self-discipline unlocks the development of talent and extends our performance to the limit.

As I teach principles of a planned life-style, people everywhere ask, "How do I discipline myself? Can I really change and learn self-discipline?"

For us the question may not be "Can people change?" We have seen people change, such as the excessive drinker who "goes on the wagon," the thief who mends his ways and seeks a life of honesty. Then there's the overweight lady who, after trying many things, finally gets control of her life and slims down to a new image of loveliness and a new wardrobe.

So our question is not "Can people change?" You have seen that happen. The question is "Can *I* change? Is it possible for me to find the motivation to alter my life as others have done?"

People do change and for three basic reasons: First, it is possible to change if you hurt badly enough. How many times have you said or heard other people say, "Wait till he hits rock bottom, then he will change"? Right now I can think of three people who have done just that. They came to the end of themselves and began to change.

Second, I have seen people change who became bored enough. I have seen Ph.D's, attorneys, and business executives who dropped out of their professions. They became bored and perhaps joined a commune or returned to a simple life in the country. One man bought a boat and sailed into the setting sun. Boredom can become a powerful thing in people's lives.

Third, it is possible to change if you believe it is possible. I discovered this one day when I read Mark 3:13-15:

> Afterwards he went up into the hills and summoned certain ones he chose, inviting them to come and join him there; and they did. Then he selected twelve of them to be his regular companions and to go out to preach and to cast out demons.

Suddenly it struck me: Jesus never calls people because of what they are but because of what He wants them to become. Thus it follows, Jesus did not call Peter because he was a fisherman but because of what He wanted him to become. Matthew was not called because he was a tax collector but because of what Jesus wanted him to become.

And so it is with us. We are all becomers. It is possible to change if we open our mind and heart to the truth. The Lord Himself has called us to a life of change and self-discipline.

2

How Completely Can A Person Change?

One day an 80-year-old man became convinced that he had received a message from God. As he was not particularly interested in giving the remaining days of his life to what he knew God wanted him to do, he began to create every excuse he could think of to show God and man why he should not get involved.

He complained loudly that he was not suited for the job God was asking him to do. His task was to be a hard one which would involve nerves of steel. His occupation had been one of a gentle nature. It had left him much time for contemplation. Although he did not like some things he had seen men do to others during his 80 years of life, he did not feel there was much he could do about it.

In his heart he now felt strange approaching people with problems and telling them God had sent him to help them. After all, God had not spoken to them about this—only to him.

He created every possible argument and excuse to avoid making this change of vocation and direction in his life. His "ace in the hole" was that to do what God wanted would require talking to politicians, national leaders, and vast crowds of people. How could he possibly do this without training or experience in the national arena?

How completely can people change? Both biblical and secular history record that our senior citizen so completely changed that he, Moses, was able to stand before the Pharaoh of Egypt and demand that the children of Israel be set free. Then he marched them to the Promised Land.

In the New Testament, lives were so altered that prostitutes sinned no more, blind people saw, and lame people walked. Thieves were forgiven and made recompense for what they had stolen.

It is possible for people of any age to change any habit. An acquaintance smoked for 57 years, from age 10 to age 67. At 67, short of breath and coughing, he visited the doctor. His doctor said he must stop smoking if he wanted any kind of later years to enjoy. He handed the doctor his cigarettes. When the message to quit came with enough authority, the motivation necessary for self-discipline surfaced within him and he quit.

People with the most difficult problems can bring their lives under control if they come to believe it is possible. Let me show you how completely people can change.

A booklet put out by a pharmaceutical house for doctors to give to overweight patients is titled "Are You Really Serious About Losing Weight?" On page eight it says:

> The total exchange of particles in our tissues each day amounts to about five percent of our body weight. In other words, a person turns over a mass of material amounting to his own body weight every 20 days. In this way, every tissue of the body—from the nails on our toes to the hair on our heads— undergoes a complete exchange of particles periodically. This continues throughout our lives. A living body in 1980 is not the same body it was in 1970.

Everything about us can change. Our bad habits can change. Our weight and physical condition can change. The mental outlook we presently carry can change.

Friendships can change. Your marriage and the problems you are experiencing can change. You do not need to live with your life out of control.

It is possible for people to bring their lives under control and for changes to be made in every area.

However, it does not happen unless we plan for it to happen—it takes self-discipline. Only by design can people bring their actions under control so their daily living bears out that their deeds "are as good as their doctrine."

After Jesus had forgiven the woman taken in adultery—"Go and sin no more"—she was now expected to make some changes in her life. The message had come with authority. When the message comes with authority, motivation for change takes place.

3

Motivated to Change

Not long ago while I was teaching a seminar, a man came up to me and said, "You have been talking about how to set and attain goals. At home in my drawer I have a file folder filled with goals and plans, but I lack the motivation. Where do I get the motivation to do what I know I should do?"

On many occasions I have sat with people, prayed and cried with them, that they learn how to discipline themselves.

You may think of out-of-control areas in your own life to bring under control because you suffer from them.

I have found that motivation revolves around importance, benefits, satisfaction, and progress.

17

Importance

I am motivated when I receive a message with authority. Often I think of the apostle Peter in John 21:15-17 when Jesus spoke to him about his capacity of love for his master. The question of the capacity of love was asked in three different ways.

The response called for was always the same: "Then do what I ask you to do." Love speaks with authority. Love is motivational because when a message comes backed by love, you know it is for real.

I knew when I fell in love. It was the day I met a lady who meant enough to me that I wanted to change things in my life which did not please her.

That lady, Mary Freleigh, is now my wife of 27 years. The need for making changes is still with me and will be all my life. The motivation remains the same. Mary means enough to me that I want to keep altering my life in order to please her. This is what I mean when I say motivation comes from a position of how important an issue is to you.

Benefits

Another means of motivation is benefits. In an area of your life you want to bring under control for the glory of God, take out pencil and paper and list the ways you will benefit when you take control of this problem.

Should you be struggling with debt, list benefits you will receive when these debts are paid. For example:

1. You will have the money to spend that you are now paying on interest.

2. You will be relieved of the pressure and bondage you feel from owing on things you have already used up.

3. You will be able to plan activities for yourself and your family that you cannot consider now.

4. There will be no more past-due notices in your mail.

5. You and your spouse can discuss plans for the future rather than haggle over past performance.

Benefits need to be listed when we consider taking control of an area of our life because benefits clearly seen become part of our motivational process.

Satisfaction

Then ask yourself if taking control of this area is satisfying. Do you feel better about yourself?

Is taking control of this area going to honor God? Will it help in your relationship with others?

For some of us satisfaction is almost an intangible. We struggle to define it. But one thing we are sure of: We know when we are dissatisfied.

With satisfaction comes a sense of pleasure. Conflict and tension are eased. When satisfied, we can accept things we cannot change and deal realistically with hard things. The apostle Paul made this clear in Philippians 4:11,12:

> Not that I was ever in need, for I have learned how to get along happily whether I have much or little. I know how to live on almost nothing or with everything. I have learned the secret of contentment in every situation.

Contentment is complete satisfaction.

Progress

There is strong motivation in seeing progress. When the area of life we have selected to bring under control starts to adjust so it is an honor to God, we are motivated to do even better.

Taking control of our weight rather than letting appetite control us becomes motivational to stepping on the scales and losing pounds.

Thus whenever we are seeking to bring something in our lives under control, we need a means to measure our progress. If you choose to control your weight, how many pounds have you lost since you started? If you choose finances, how much have you saved toward a purchase, or how much debt have you retired?

Going over the progress will become highly motivational to you!

Motivation for action comes from the *importance* of the issue, the *benefits* of the change, the *satisfaction* we find personally in the change, and the *progress* we see in life as we are going through this change.

4

Actions That Bring About Change

I have found that people *want* to make changes in their lives. The man who loses his temper and makes a fool of himself at home or at work does not enjoy being like that. He would like to change.

A person struggling with work habits that keep him from top performance wants to be able to control his time, energy, and output so he can do his best.

Those of us who struggle with a poor self-image long to change how we view ourselves so we can feel worthy to exercise our gifts.

One reason many of us do not change is because we do not *plan* to change. Things don't just happen. We may think that we are victims of circumstances, but most of the time we are victims of the circumstances created by a person who exercises self-discipline by planning.

Let's think about this for a moment.

Many who struggle with credit debt are the victims of someone else's plan. Depending on the survey you read, you and I are exposed to 300 to 1500 advertisements per day.

Radio, television, newspapers, magazines, billboards, displays—even clowns standing on the corner in front of a business—are attempting to get us to buy.

We have all fallen victim to advertising. I have purchased products I did not need and did not want after some advertiser made me hungry to buy.

Advertising is a calculated, creative, funded plan to raise our level of desire for a product. If the product is expensive enough, such as a car, large boat, or several products bought on the easy-payment plan, we find ourselves suddenly in debt.

The debt has not come simply because we are undisciplined, though we may be. It is not due totally to our impetuous nature, though many of us have one. We are in part the end product of some retail businessman's advertising plan.

Changing Our Lives Requires a Plan

The best way I know to stop being the product of someone else's plan is to have a plan of my own. To build such a plan requires pencil and paper. Change has started in my life when my pencil touches the paper.

Let's face it, advertisers do influence us and they do not carry their ideas around in their heads. The ideas are put on paper, critiqued, organized, prioritized, and set into motion.

Before any plan begins, the wise person writes out the purpose of what he is doing. A statement of purpose is simply a written statement of why we are going to start what we are about to do.

But you might ask: "What if I don't make a good plan?" My answer to you is "Any plan is better than no plan."

Once we know why we are going to do what it is we are going to do, we need to outline the steps we will follow to cause what we want done to happen.

I keep telling myself that I need to face facts. Things don't just happen—somebody plans them.

Tonight I am having a dinner party for two men I want to introduce to each other. For their work and futures' sake these men need to meet. They come from different areas of the country and different philosophies. However, because of what they are both doing they can greatly benefit one another. Should a relationship grow and they be able to help one another, they may say one day, "Wasn't it fortunate we met at Lanson's home?" In truth they met because somebody planned to get them together.

Any time we want change, we need to write out why (the purpose of the change), list the steps we will do to bring about the change, then prioritize these steps and give them some time reference. Now we have a plan for change.

We are today what we have been becoming, so if we are not happy with what we are, then we need to set in motion a plan to become something different in the future.

5

A Key to Change

A key principle to making changes in life is not to program yourself for failure.

There are many ways people program themselves to fail. The chief one is that they try to do too much. Do not attempt to build a strong devotional time, curb your temper, stop smoking, and overcome procrastination all at the same time.

If you try such a Herculean task, you will fail. You will fail not because you cannot change, but because you have set up a program that assures you will fail.

We do this all the time. For years I felt so unworthy and such a failure that anytime I would think about getting my life under control I would set up a program of improvement that was so all-encompassing that I would fail. It was such a problem to me that I only felt comfortable with failure.

When we want to make a change, we need to pick one thing and set up and prioritize a plan to start and continue the change.

Solomon said in Proverbs 16:9, "We should make plans—counting on God to direct us." Paul the apostle told us we are called to a life of change when he wrote in Philippians 1:6:

> And I am sure that God who began the good work within you will keep right on helping you grow in his grace until his task within you is finally finished on that day when Jesus Christ returns.

People need to bring their lives under control through self-discipline as an honor to God. To accomplish this, start small and master one area before you move on to another.

Another way we program ourselves for failure is to demand change in everything. There are some things about each of us that can never be changed. I cannot make myself shorter or narrower—thinner, yes; narrower, no.

There is no way for me to change things I have already done. As a father, husband, worker, and employer I have struggled with my own set of problems. Not everything I have done has been good, nor has every decision I have ever made been the best one, or even a good one.

But I cannot change history. What is done is done. I must accept that and its consequences. I program myself for change when I recognize that what cannot be changed must be accepted, and that I must simply go on living.

I program myself for failure when I assume everything I do must be perfect. As you seek to build self-discipline into your life, think about this: You are after progress, not perfection.

My wife and I sometimes fuss about things we do that bother each other. The truth of the matter is it is usually something I do that bothers her. My best defense is to point out I have been working on that, and help her to see I have made progress, though I have not attained perfection.

This reminds me of the old preacher who was holding a meeting and making the point that all men are sinners. To emphasize this truth he said, "If there is any man here who has never done anything wrong, stand up."

To his utter amazement one man stood on the back row. The preacher asked, "Do you mean to say, sir, you have never done anything wrong?"

The man replied, "Pastor, I've done plenty

wrong, but I'm standing in proxy for my wife's first husband."

The most exciting days in my life are the days change is taking place. When I am struggling along in a routine, accepting things I know could be and should be different, life is a problem.

Are you desiring change in your life? Then choose one area of your life, make a plan to change what needs changing, and aggressively pursue your plan.

II

EXPLORING
SELF-DISCIPLINE

6

Is Self-Discipline Selfish?

Not long ago someone came to me during a break at one of my seminars and started asking all kinds of questions about self-discipline.

I had been speaking on altering self-image and setting and attaining personal and family goals. The more this person talked, the more apparent it became that he had a self-esteem problem. Many times he set goals but did not follow through with a program to attain them.

The bottom line was he was not sure it was good to follow through on a plan of self-improvement. He said self-improvement smacked of self-glorification. If you worked at any self-improvement program it would massage your ego, which we all agree is not a good thing—an ego out of control.

Suddenly I realized these were all just words. The real issue was that he did not want to exercise self-discipline. He was looking for some rationalization for why he was not working at some of the issues in his life that needed correcting.

One thing 48 years of living has taught me is that every person has problems. Life is like that. Each one of us faces our own storms. We are each seeking to keep our sails trimmed and our boats on course as a storm brews somewhere in our lives.

One of the amazing things about living is that many of our storms are the result of contrary winds which we invite into our lives. If we do not invite them in, we at least leave the door open because the breeze feels good. Before we know it the breeze has turned into a storm and we seem unable to get the door shut against the blast.

Solomon in his wisdom wrote in Proverbs 25:28, "A man without self-control is as defenseless as a city with broken-down walls."

The man talking to me at the seminar was trying to tell me he did not want to exercise self-control because he would be glorifying self. In actuality, just the opposite is true.

Self-control and self-discipline are concerted

efforts of the will to bring the self to a controlled position.

Speaking to His followers, Jesus Christ made one thing clear: A person could not do what he himself wanted and what Jesus wanted him to do at the same time. Jesus Christ is keenly aware of the battle everyone faces in keeping control of self when He said, "If anyone wants to be a follower of Mine, let him deny himself and take up his cross and follow Me."

Down through history men have indicated that their greatest battles were not of the enemy without, but rather of the enemies within.

In sports we hear about the need for mental toughness. Businessmen discuss constantly the need to find committed people to work with them. People in the arts speak of being dedicated to excellence. Ministers and Christian leaders call for us to make sacrifices and be willing to serve other people.

None of this happens unless we deal realistically with the problem of disciplining ourselves to do what we know we ought to do.

Too many times in my life I have said about some particular activity, "I could do that if I wanted to, but..." I only told a half-truth. What I really meant was I did not want to exercise the self-discipline necessary to perform as needed to reap the personal benefit from the exercise of self-discipline.

We have all been guilty of this kind of rationalization; today we call it copping out. But let's start changing our patterns. Let's expose ourselves to the truth. Self-discipline is not a glorification of self as my friend tried to tell me. It is a calculated act of our will to do what we know we should do.

So the issue today should not be, "I have my own life to live so I'm going to do it my way." Rather, we should be saying, "God has given me this life for a purpose. I am going to control my selfish wishes and live it right!"

7

Is Self-Discipline
A Form of Bondage?

High achievers are goal-oriented people. This is true because when a person becomes goal-oriented he focuses his ability and energy on an objective. During the teaching I do on a planned life-style, I encourage people to set goals each year in six areas of their lives: spiritual, social, family, financial, physical, and mental.

In order to accomplish a goal it becomes necessary to exercise self-discipline to follow through on the plan we have set in motion. Some of us are able to choose a goal, write it down, and even outline a plan to meet our objective. But we tell ourselves, "I can never meet a goal. I just lack the willpower."

What we are really saying is we do not want to choose the path of self-discipline which will lead us to the top of our mountain of decision.

In my 30 years of sharing ideas with people, I remain amazed how many people get the idea that goals and self-discipline are some kind of legalistic trap that puts a person into bondage.

Nothing could be farther from the truth.

I am a sailor by hobby. Had I been born a hundred years ago, I might have been a sailor by vocation. There is no experience quite like the crack of a sail when you change course in a 25-knot wind.

Sailing is only as good an experience as you make of it. Sit in front of the television, neglect your vessel, and she will be tied to the dock while others are enjoying a good sail or even a cruise. Do your maintenance in a haphazard manner, and when you need a piece of gear it might fail you for lack of attention.

Keeping your boat in shape takes some work and consistent effort. For a larger boat, even a maintenance plan or schedule needs to be created and followed. To create such a schedule and work at keeping your vessel maintained is the very thing that frees you to sail when you want to go.

Life is very much the same way. Self-discipline is what keeps us on top of things. It is what enables us to accomplish tasks. Why do we hear it said so often, "If you want something done, go to a busy person"? The truth is that often busy people are self-disciplined people who have learned to control themselves so they can make their time productive. One thing we all have in equal measure is time. We are not all equal in intellect, strength, or artistic, musical, or mechanical aptitude, but we all get the same number of hours in a day.

The self-disciplined person is able to make his work hours count. His work hours are filled with accomplishment. In this way he or she is free to fill leisure hours with activities he enjoys.

We sometimes forget that not everyone at the beach is having a good time. Not everyone at Disneyland is happy. Maybe for the moment, but if they did not have their business taken care of, their affairs in order, their finances lined up before they arrived for vacation, their time away could be a time of bondage because they are not free to enjoy themselves.

Self-discipline is a freeing activity. It does not take time from you but enables you to accomplish tasks so your free time is really free.

There seems to be a feeling that to do nothing is the pinnacle of freedom. The trouble with doing nothing is that you never know when you're finished. Experience tells me that the route to freedom is self-discipline. The path to bondage is a lack of self-discipline, a lack of accomplishment which creates bondage to pressure from being behind in things we want to do.

8

Is Self-Discipline A Biblical Concept?

When I was asked recently to join a couple for lunch, I did not realize that for one hour I was going to verbally battle what has become an attitude all too prevalent in today's churches.

No sooner had we exchanged greetings than they began to tell me about a relative, a young man who has a drinking problem. During the conversation it became clear to me the young man does have a problem which has kept him from earning a livelihood for his young wife who is about to give birth to their first child. My friends were blaming the drinking for the problem, but it appeared to me that drinking was an escape from the fact this young man was not willing to discipline himself to accept responsibility for his actions.

The young man attends church and continually asks God's forgiveness and deliverance from his problems.

After an hour of conversation I left them with this thought to ponder: The gospel of Jesus Christ is not an experience which makes us less responsible for our actions, but it actually makes us more responsible for our actions.

The New Testament is saturated with the challenge to discipline ourselves and bring our lives under control.

Titus 2:11,12 states:

> For the free gift of salvation is now being offered to everyone; and along with this gift comes the realization that God wants us to turn from godless living and sinful pleasures to live good, God-fearing lives day after day.

Here Paul clearly instructs those who receive God's free salvation to work at the job of living lives that honor the Lord. They are told that God wants them to turn from godless living day after day. This does not just happen—we must exercise self-discipline to take control of our lives for the glory of God.

The need for self-discipline is evident in 2 Peter 2:9,10:

> So also the Lord can rescue you and me from the temptations that surround us, and continue to punish the ungodly until the day of final judgment comes. He is especially hard on those who follow their own evil, lustful thoughts, and those who are proud and willful, daring even to scoff at the Glorious Ones without so much as trembling.

Paul states in 1 Corinthians 10:13:

> But remember this—the wrong desires that come into your life aren't anything new and different. Many others have faced exactly the same problems before you. And no temptation is irresistible. You can trust God to keep the temptation from becoming so strong that you can't stand up against it, for he has promised this and will do what he says. He will show you how to escape temptation's power so that you can bear up patiently against it.

Both Paul and Peter are saying that God makes it possible for us to stand against temptations. This

means not just fleshly desires but the temptation of slothfulness as well as the temptation
to procrastinate and to succumb to all manner
of things every day that limit our productivity for
God.

Both Paul and Peter tell us God provides the
way out and the power over temptation if we
avail ourselves of it. Peter said that God is hard
on those who are proud and follow their own will,
while Paul's words are, "He will show you how
to escape temptation's power."

Our Lord Himself spoke to the issue of self-
discipline when He said to the woman taken in
adultery in John 8:10,11:

> "Where are your accusers? Didn't
> even one of them condemn you?" "No
> Sir," she said. And Jesus said, "Neither
> do I. Go and sin no more."

This woman was forgiven and told to accept
responsibility for her actions. She was told to
exercise self-discipline and not continue in the
same life-style she had previously.

Jesus told the man who was healed at the pool
of Bethesda to practice self-discipline:

> But afterwards Jesus found him in
> the temple and told him, "Now you are
> well; don't sin as you did before, or

something even worse may happen to you (John 5:14)."

God does not exonerate us from responsibility for our lives. To embrace the Lord Jesus means we have found a Friend who died for us when we had no good thought about Him. That truth alone ought to call out of us an effort of self-discipline so our lives honor Him.

Accepting the responsibility for our actions is never an easy thing. Self-discipline, denial of self, and self-control are never easy, but they are biblical.

9

Self-Discipline and Surrender

In the church, believers are taught to surrender their will to the will of God. Often they are quoted a passage such as Galatians 2:20:

> I have been crucified with Christ; and it is no longer I who live, but Christ lives in me; and the life which I now live in the flesh I live by faith in the Son of God, who loved me, and delivered Himself up for me (NASB).

Such passages have been taken to mean that man is to have no control over his life. "Surrender yourself to the will of God, serve Him, and He will never leave you or forsake you" is what we are told that the Scriptures teach. The question is, What is meant by surrender?

Too many times we have interpreted surrender to mean we do not need to pay the price of self-control—we simply surrender to God and all our problems become His problems. I often use the illustration of the overweight person who goes to the altar or the room of prayer and surrenders his fat to God. But God does not want someone's fat—He wants him to do something about it.

One great problem in self-discipline is how to reconcile the surrendering of the will to God and the need to be responsible for our actions. We make a mistake when we use the principle of surrender to cop out of our personal responsibility to live right.

It is time to think through again how to live the Christian life. For the gospel of Jesus Christ to be attractive to the unbelieving person, it cannot be some sort of idea where a person abdicates responsibility for his actions. Christians are often looked on as weak people because they must lean on God to solve all their problems. As believers you and I know this is not true, but to the unbelieving person this appears to be the case.

When it comes to living out the forgiveness experience, Jesus expects man to exercise self-discipline so his life can be a symphony of praise to God. Take a simple verse like Philippians 4:13: "I can do all things through Him who strengthens me (NASB)." This is not a statement of Jesus *or* me doing all things. It is a statement of Jesus *and* me doing all things.

In wedding the need for self-discipline and surrender in living the Christian life, the thing that we need to do is set our will to do what is right and then surrender our set will to Jesus for the strength to keep it set. For some believers this will be a new experience. For years they have been fleeing to God and giving Him the responsibility to set their wills. When they fail it appears as if God has failed. They get the impression that God is not doing for them what He promised.

Read Philippians 4:13 again: "I CAN DO all things THROUGH CHRIST who strengthens me." The Christian's life of self-discipline is a team effort. It is you and the Lord each doing your part.

10

Is Self-Discipline Inherited or Learned?

At a recent seminar of mine, one of the attendees said, "Lanson, it is all well and good for you to talk about self-discipline because it is so easy for you." I laughed and tried to communicate to this fellow that self-discipline was a struggle for me just as it is for him. Nothing I said seemed to convince him.

But it is true—self-discipline is very hard for me. I am not by nature a disciplined person. This may be one of the reasons I think about it and discuss it so much with people. It is hard for me, and the only way I make any progress in a disciplined life-style is to keep it in front of me as one of the primary issues to solve in my life.

I know me. I have looked at myself when I

have been grossly overweight. I quit weighing myself at 255 pounds because I did not want to know anymore what I did weigh. I have carried projects in my briefcase for months because I could not seem to make myself sit down and do them.

For years I made shallow public presentations because I could not exercise the self-discipline necessary to study. When I was answering April and May's mail in November, I would not exactly say I was self-disciplined!

I have been guilty of all of the above and more. Finally, I decided there is no such thing as self-discipline genes. The ability to discipline oneself is not inherited, but rather is a learned activity.

Now I do think part of the learning process can take place early in a person's life if he is surrounded by good adult role models. Most of our learning at an early age comes from observation.

My grandson, two-and-a-half, is an avid football fan. Last fall when his dad watched the football games on television, my grandson had on a child's army helmet and, using a balloon for a ball, was running and falling on the floor. When his dad asked what he was doing, he said that he was playing football.

After a few weeks we noticed he would run and fall and then he would get up again and try to do the same thing in slow motion. Suddenly it dawned on us that he saw the instant replays in slow motion on the television and through observation alone he thought this was part of the game.

During the Super Bowl I noticed he would get down with his ball (I had given him a football for Christmas) when the players lived up on television. When the ball was hiked, he would pick up his ball and run or throw it.

Without being taught, this young boy had learned several things about football. His knowledge was picked up through observation alone and then put into practice.

Those who have had self-disciplined parents have the advantage of an empirical data bank in their minds that tells them how self-disciplined people conduct themselves. But they must either reject or emulate what they see. There are no self-discipline genes for you and me anymore than there are football genes for my grandson.

If self-discipline were easy, then it would not be a problem. We would not be discussing it here. The fact is, in some areas of life, we all struggle with an unruly will.

But this is no different than it has ever been in history. It is said of Victor Hugo he had such a problem with self-discipline that when he wrote he would have his servant lock him in his bedroom without clothes and bring him his meals. In this way he could not go out and thus, without anything else to do and no way to escape to another place, he would force himself to write.

I thought I was the only one with that kind of self-discipline problem! When I wrote my first book the only way I could discipline myself to do it was to go to a friend's house 2,000 miles away.

I took with me only what I needed to write the book. There was no phone. I had no car, and the home was not within walking distance of any store or shopping center. Only then could I discipline myself to complete the writing of the book.

I felt badly that I was such an undisciplined person, until I heard about Victor Hugo. I at least kept my clothes on when I wrote.

Self-discipline is a learned activity. It is a skill that can be developed just as you can learn to play an instrument or further an athletic skill.

III

PRESCRIPTION
FOR SELF-DISCIPLINE

11

How to Begin Exercising Self-Discipline

Now we come to the heart of the issue: "How do I begin exercising self-discipline?"

As one friend put it, "How do I discipline myself to begin disciplining myself, so I can exercise self-discipline?" I thought of the song which was popular a few years ago. The lyrics said, "I was looking back to see if she was looking back to see if I was looking back to see if she was looking back at me."

In thinking about where to start learning self-discipline, I find one of the most difficult things is locating the end of the string so there is some place to start. Self-discipline is not much different from anything else we do. Starting seems to be the difficult part.

Have you ever picked up a fishing line or a snarl of string that was so tangled you could not free an end to begin working? I have a solution for you the next time that happens: Take a pair of scissors and cut the string. Now you have two ends. Take either one of the ends and get to work unraveling.

Self-discipline is somewhat the same way.

First, do not dwell on your lack of self-discipline. Do not try to justify any future problem you may have because you can point to some problems you have had in the past. Now is the time to lay the past to rest—there is nothing you can do about it. However, the past can affect you negatively if you have not been successful in your efforts at self-discipline.

Next, do not look at all the self-discipline problems you face. My advice is to not try to face all these problems at once. "Divide and conquer" instead. Pick one thing in one area of your life which you want to bring under control and go to work on that one thing.

Then try what I do. Take out pencil and paper. At the top of the paper write down the area of your life, issue, or problem you are going to deal with through self-discipline.

Next, list the circumstances which hinder your coping with the problem. If it is a weight problem, do you snack when frustrated? Do you reward yourself with sweets? Is your struggle with eating out or entertaining, or perhaps with being entertained?

Now write down when these difficult times come. Are there certain hours of the day, days of the week, or events that trigger your self-discipline problem?

Perhaps you do quite well on the job but, when you get home, you let your guard down and fall into a habit with the paper, popcorn, and television and do not accomplish what you want to do in your leisure time. A step forward in beginning self-discipline is to write those things out so you can see the problem objectively on paper, not just subjectively in your mind.

Something happens to me when I get struggles inside of me down on paper. It seems as if I now have a problem I can deal with. I have a beginning, a size, and a dimension that I can see and identify. As long as it stays in my mind, I keep going around and around, arguing with myself why I am so weak and cannot get on with the job.

I was encouraged for weeks and months to begin a daily radio program. As long as it remained in my mind, I kept finding reasons to tell myself I could never do the work and preparation necessary to produce it.

Then one day, tired of the procrastination, I took out paper and pencil and wrote down what needed to be done daily in order to make five broadcasts a week. The more I wrote the more I realized the time to do this work was available. I would have to rearrange priorities, leave out some things that were not very important to begin with, and discipline myself.

The self-discipline to do the broadcast was not the issue once I took out pencil and paper and moved the issue out of my mind so I could deal with it. As long as it remained in my mind it was like the ball of string where I could not find the end. Putting pencil to paper was like cutting the string. Now I had a place to start.

So to break the habit of no self-discipline, take out paper and pencil and select one thing you are going to deal with and forget the past. Don't look at everything you want to change—just the one thing. Note the circumstances under which you struggle and the times when they happen. Now you have a problem you can solve.

Where does self-discipline start? With pencil and paper.

12

Plan Ahead

Most people who struggle with self-discipline are in a battle of the will because they never planned to be any different. Strange as it may sound you will never be a self-disciplined person unless you plan to take control of your life.

As I pointed out, one of the most important tools to stimulate you in a lasting experience of self-discipline is paper and pencil. A car begins to move when you put the transmission into gear. The only way I can explain what happens to me is, when the pencil touches the paper and begins to move, it puts my brain into gear.

As long as I carry things around in my mind, I keep discovering reasons I cannot do something. Once I have transferred what I want to do to paper, my motivation for accomplishment increases sharply. If I put the need or goal down on paper, I become a positive achiever.

Some people have the wisdom to plan but never do so because they are unsure they will build a good plan. I have a wise friend who taught me to state the problem and make a plan, no matter how weak it might seem and start working out the plan. This has proven to be an excellent piece of advice for me. Often when I start dealing with the plan my enthusiasm grows; my creativity appears to move up a notch and success comes as I am led to improve the plan, change it, or make a new one altogether.

Some weeks ago it became apparent I had to gather some friends around me if I was going to do all I should be doing in my work of helping people and honoring God. I made a simple plan. Write five letters per day, hand-written, because I am seeking quality, not quantity. My need is for 100 people who will join me in praying for and helping in seminars.

Have you ever tried to write five letters every day, six days per week? It is a real grind. My inclination with tasks like this is to put it off as long as possible. So I made a plan. I wrote a basic letter which is three paragraphs long. It is of such a nature it can be changed to fit each individual but they all get a hand-written letter with the same basic message.

Next I wrote a status report which when typed covered two sides of an 8½ x 11 sheet of paper. Then I copied 100 of these. Next I took a good letter of testimonial and made 100 copies. I put each into a file of its own. Then I counted out 100 return envelopes and 100 response cards for the people to send back. Finally, I counted out 110 pieces of stationery and 110 envelopes (this allows for mistakes in writing an address or name).

Now each of these pieces is in a file folder of its own. They are all in my briefcase with a supply of five pens gathered together by a rubber band.

One of my first activities each day is to go to the briefcase, take out five of each item, select addresses of my friends and those I hope will become my friends, and sit down and start writing.

This has been a successful program for me because I do not have to hunt what I need for the work. It is all in one place because I planned it that way. Nothing is more discouraging than to try and work and not be able to locate what you need to do the job. Also, when I sit to do the letters there is nothing to distract me. The only thing out in front of me is what I need to complete the task.

I know exactly how much I have to do. There

is an end stated before I start. My project is five a day.

Speaking of five a day, here is a key for me— not 30 per week, but five a day. If I think about 30 per week, I will try to put it off as long as I can and I will never get it done because 30 hand-written letters in a week would be an unwanted task.

The kind of thing I did in building a satisfactory plan to write 30 letters by hand per week by writing five per day is an exercise in self-discipline. When I go on a plane, that briefcase is with me. If I babysit my grandson for a few days, the briefcase remains visible because this is my program.

So . . . take some task you have been putting off. Get out your paper and pencil and write down what it is you want to do. Then outline steps as they come to you. Control starts with the decision to begin.

13

Focus on Fewer Things

I want to tell you about one of the great sins in my life. No, it is not bank robbery or chasing my neighbor's wife. I have not shot anyone, nor have I been in an assault and battery attack. The biggest sin in my life is having periods of unproductivity.

My lack of self-discipline is sometimes appalling to me. To quote one fellow, "I'm not afraid of work. Sometimes I lay right down beside it and go to sleep."

I am 48 years old and this has been a lifelong struggle with me. There are periods when it seems as if there is no end to what I can accomplish. At other times, work—important, creative work—will lay on my desk and the pile just gets higher.

When this happens I get so discouraged that despair hits. These are the times I want to quit. At these unproductive moments I will quickly accept additional work or responsibility. Many times I find myself agreeing to almost anything in these low moments. These new tasks are then heaped on the old ones and my enthusiasm is further quenched.

The only way I had found to solve this dilemma is by a vigorous assault on fewer things. To restore my faith and get moving again, I take one task and complete it, then take another and work on it. By doing one thing at a time my sense of accomplishment returns. My spirit of attainment rises. The joy of feeling productive begins to return.

For my life to be of benefit to my family, to others, and an honor to God, I have sought ways to make the productive periods longer and the unproductive periods shorter.

Perhaps my new effort at self-discipline is because after 48 years I know what I can do. With the rest of my life the decision has been made to do what I can do and do the best I can for God and man.

In the endeavor to gain a self-disciplined lifestyle, try what I have learned after years of frustration—focus on fewer things.

At a recent seminar, a man told me that there was so much information, so many principles to act upon, and such a volume of things he could do to alter his life-style that it was like trying to get a drink from a fire hydrant.

I have heard the same kind of comment many times before. Always at the close of the seminar I tell people they have enough information to set personal and family goals, to start a budget, to alter their self-image, etc. Then I warn them that the biggest mistake they can possibly make is to go home and try to work on all of those things at once. They need to select one or, at the most, two things and work on them until they are part of their life. Next they should select one or two others and work on them.

From experience, I know that the person who goes home and tries to change everything simultaneously will end up abandoning most, if not all, of his attempts at self-discipline.

Previously, the challenge was made to take pencil and paper and make a plan in the area of your life where you are struggling for self-discipline.

You might be struggling with weight, lack of exercise, procrastination of details, catching up on correspondence, being disciplined about flossing your teeth, and 20 other things. Whatever you do, do not write them all down and draft a plan to be corrective in all of these at once.

Try too much and chances are you will do nothing.

Instead, take step two in the prescription for self-discipline: Focus on one or two areas and work on them until they become part of your life.

14

Eliminate the Unimportant

Next in the prescription for self-control I challenge you to eliminate the unnecessary and obsolete in your life.

In an old story, a farmer told his wife this was the day to plow the "south forty." He started early to oil the tractor. Needing more oil, he went to the shop to get it.

On the way he noticed the pigs were not fed so he went to the corn crib where he found some sacks. That reminded him the potatoes were sprouting. He started for the potato pit. As he passed the woodpile, he remembered his wife wanted wood in the house. As he picked up a few sticks, an ailing chicken passed. He dropped the wood and reached for the chicken. When evening arrived, he still had not gotten the tractor to the field—and so time goes.

A motion picture of many an executive's morning would reveal that he too finds it difficult to get to the "south forty." He hangs his hat in the cloakroom. On the way to his office he meets a colleague and chats or sticks his head in a friend's office to tell him about the dinner party the night before. When he gets to his desk, the briefcase which he took home and brought back unopened has to be emptied. From it he takes several time-consumers he was going to read last night. He glances over these magazines and advertisements and then gets curious about the morning mail. A couple of letters catch his fancy. They do not need to be dealt with until next week but he starts here—so time goes.

Many of us identify with both of these stories. One of the best pieces of advice I could give you on self-discipline is to eliminate the unnecessary and obsolete.

Paul the apostle spoke such a message in Philippians:

> No, dear brothers, I am still not all I should be but I am bringing all my energies to bear on this one thing: Forgetting the past and looking forward to what lies ahead, I strain to reach the end of the race and receive the prize for which God is calling us up to

heaven because of what Christ did for us. Dear brothers, pattern your lives after mine and notice who else lives up to my example. For I have told you often before, and I say it again now with tears in my eyes, there are many who walk along the Christian road who are really enemies of the cross of Christ. Their future is eternal loss, for their god is their appetite: they are proud of what they should be ashamed of; and all they think about is life here on earth. But our homeland is in heaven, where our Savior, the Lord Jesus Christ is; and we are looking forward to his return from there (Philippians 3:13,14,17-20).

In these words Paul is outlining the need to eliminate the unimportant in our lives. He admits his own need to keep striving to live the best possible life. He tells us he has focused his energies on one thing: to reach forward to attain the prize at the end of the race of life. He outlines for us the unimportant when he says that too many people give themselves totally to this life. His statement is, "They are proud of what they should be ashamed of; and all they think about is life here on earth."

In my own life I have struggled with choosing between the necessary and the unimportant. One thing I have noticed: If a project sits for a while, it might actually be unimportant or even obsolete. For example, as I travel on planes I will quite often read magazines, including the advertisements. Quite often I will clip things out that I think I want, need, or think would be fun to have. I then toss these into my briefcase. After finishing the trip and emptying my work out of the case, I will look over these coupons I have clipped. At that point, 99 times out of 100 I will throw them away. What seemed important on the plane is unimportant ten days later.

If you have something you are doing which seems important but when you come back to it later it has become unimportant, do not clutter your life with it. Lay it aside. You may have outgrown the need for it. In the light of your own personal progress there are things which become obsolete.

As you go about plowing the south forty today, keep the task in focus. Choose not to be sidetracked by activities or people.

Eliminate from your schedule things that are unimportant, concentrate on a few things, and do them one at a time according to your predetermined plan.

15

Guard Your Time

Across my desk comes a constant flow of pamphlets advertising seminars on time management, decision-making, investing, and a host of self-improvement activities.

In bookstores, Christian and secular, there are entire sections dedicated to helping people deal with their personal problems. You can subscribe to magazines which are designed to motivate people. In airports are racks of cassette tapes and now videotapes which can be purchased and used as positive input into a person's life.

Much of this material stems from a money-oriented context and is the product of humanistic thinkers who believe man is in charge of his own destiny. Some of the material we do not want in our lives because the end results are materialistic and the motivation is humanistic.

However, I encourage you to listen to people who are attempting to teach people how to discipline themselves and get their lives under control. My concern is that too many people are throwing out the baby with the bathwater. Because we do not agree with a person's motivation, theology, or personal focus, we tend to reject everything he says.

There is much that Bishop Fulton Sheen and I do not agree on, but I do find challenge and help in his statement, "The mind is like a clock that is constantly running down and it needs to be wound up every day with good thoughts." This is a good, motivating, and fitting statement.

Not too long ago a pastor told me he could not have me teach in his church because I used the statement of Bishop Sheen in my book and thus he could not recommend the material. His people missed learning how to set annual spiritual goals, social goals, family goals, and physical goals. They lost out on a teaching that would lead them to budget and get their financial house in order because of one quote in a 165-page book. This is throwing out the baby with the bathwater.

As you seek to take control of your life for the glory of God, be willing to read, listen, learn, and try many things. Different authors suggest various ways to motivate and organize yourself. No two people are exactly alike. Some of what I am saying will be an encouragement and put enthusiasm in some listeners. Other people will be unaffected —maybe even turned off.

What we need to do is try lots of systems. Take a suggestion and see if it works to help you discipline yourself to make the best use of your time. If it does not help, throw it out and try something else—but do not stop trying. Life is far too short to stop trying.

When we get down to self-discipline we are dealing with activities and time. Time is very important. It is the one thing we all have in common—24 hours each day. No matter what we do we cannot manufacture more than 24 hours in our day.

On the death of Douglas Southall Freeman— long-time editor of the *Richmond Newsleader*, radio commentator, lecturer, director of a foundation and three corporations, and author of 11 volumes of distinguished biography—the *New York Times* commented that the genius of the man lay in almost inhuman self-discipline. He always had a sign on the clock over his desk so every visitor would see it. The sign read: "Time alone is irreplaceable; don't waste it."

People of accomplishment are people of self-discipline because they have such a respect for the importance of time.

Thomas Edison, the inventive genius said,

"Invention is 10 percent inspiration and 90 percent perspiration." He also redefined time: "Time cannot be measured in seconds, minutes, or hours—only in tasks accomplished." So it follows that we need to stop asking what time it is and start asking what we have gotten done.

This is a biblical principle—the importance of time. Ephesians 5:14-17 says:

> "Awake, O sleeper, and rise up from the dead; and Christ shall give you light." So be careful how you act; these are difficult days. Don't be fools; be wise: make the most of every opportunity you have for doing good. Don't act thoughtlessly but try to find out and do whatever the Lord wants you to do.

The King James version of verses 15 and 16 says, "See then that ye walk circumspectly, not as fools but as wise, redeeming the time."

When we speak of self-discipline we are talking about the proper use of time. There are people who have learned how to make good use of their time. Listen to them, read their books, and try many things until you find what satisfies you so you are doing the best you can with what God has given you.

16

Accept Constructive Criticism

It was at age 40 when some of the most dramatic changes began to take place in my life. They came as a result of the advice given me by a man for whom I have great respect.

Interestingly, the advice did not come in simple words of encouragement. The advice came as an admonition to accept responsibility for my actions and to make alterations in areas of my life where I was lacking.

My friend had correctly perceived that in certain areas in my life I was immature. He also realized that I was not willing to face this truth. In fact, it was obvious to him I had been ducking the truth about myself for years.

In his wisdom he understood I had limited the

use God could make of me because I was not mature enough to develop and use to the fullest the gifts God had given me.

It was painful for me when my friend made me face the truth about myself. What made it so painful was that he not only told me the truth about myself, but he would not let me off the hook. Each time I tried to explain away my problems as being someone else's fault, he would rebuke me. He kept me facing my problems.

When I would attempt to explain how I was a victim of circumstances, that things in my life were beyond my control, he would confront me with the truth. Since this experience I have begun to understand that the ministry of love is not simply telling people all the good things about themselves, but is helping them to face the problems in their lives and to do something about them.

King Solomon tells us about the worth of advice and constructive criticism:

> If you profit from constructive criticism you will be elected to the wise men's hall of fame. But to reject criticism is to harm yourself and your own best interests (Proverbs 15:31,32).

Solomon again exhorts us to listen to advice:

> Get all the advice you can and be
> wise the rest of your life (Proverbs
> 19:20).

Real friendship demands honesty. Each of us
has many acquaintances but few real friends.

As I was writing this manuscript I was talking
to a man who calls me a friend and I also look
to him as a friend. He was facing some difficult
times due to the rejection of his leadership in a
ministry which has claimed over 20 years of his
life. As a result of these things, he was considering a move to a new position.

He sat with me for several hours and took me
through the details of his rejection by a board
he himself had picked. There were tears in
his eyes as he walked through the hurt that had
come to him and his wife, both emotionally and
spiritually.

Then he said to me, "Lanson, I wanted to talk
to you because you have always been enough
of a friend to tell me the truth about myself and
help me face it." This was a deeply moving
moment to me because this is what growth and
change are all about.

The ministry of exhortation is when you help
people face the truth and do something about
it. To help bring about change in your life, be
willing to seek out a friend whom you love and
who loves you enough to help point out your

problems and challenge you to do something about them.

They may not be able to tell you what to do about the problem, but once you face the fact you have a problem and determine to solve it, you will come to a truth which will bring alteration and change to your life.

Again it was Solomon who said:

> If you refuse criticism you will end in poverty and disgrace; if you accept criticism you are on the road to fame (Proverbs 13:18).

People can help bring about change in our lives if we are willing to accept advice and criticism. We must not destroy ourselves by taking everything personally and becoming angry when people try to help us. Not every criticism is valid or worthwhile, but criticism is always worth considering in light of our own struggles and need for change.

Proverbs 25:11 says, "Timely advice is as lovely as golden apples in a silver basket." Let's pray for one another that we will be mature enough to receive advice and criticism.

17

Drive a Stake

In Proverbs 27:12 Solomon says:

A sensible man watches for problems
ahead and prepares to meet them. The
simpleton never looks, and suffers the
consequences.

Again Solomon shows his wisdom in Proverbs
28:13:

A man who refuses to admit his mistakes can never be successful. But if he
confesses and forsakes them, he gets
another chance.

In both statements Solomon is encouraging us to measure ourselves and be willing to admit when we have a problem and then deal with it.

For some people the hardest part of making correction in their life is admitting they have a problem. Solomon says admitting mistakes is both sensible and wise.

I will never forget Memorial Day in 1970. My two boys were 7 and 9. We were sailing on the Willamette River near where its mouth enters into the Columbia. We sailed past an open boat of about 20 feet in length. There were five adults and two children in the boat. They had the cover off the engine and were alternately jerking the pull rope, cursing, and tinkering with the engine.

Being under sail it was easy to sail over to them and speak with them as I had no engine noise to contend with. I hailed them and asked if they needed help. The river was full of debris from the spring runoff and was moving rapidly. Kindly, I attempted to point out that they were drifting rapidly toward some rocks. Did they have oars or an anchor? I asked. "No, leave us alone," was their reply. I noticed one of the men's wives was working him over verbally. She was angry because the engine would not run and mad because her husband was drunk.

We were about 100 feet away when my oldest son said, "Dad, that man just threw his wife into the water." I looked and, sure enough, his wife was just coming to the surface. Instead of getting back into the boat, she turned and started swimming for shore about a quarter of a mile away.

With the swift current and the cold temperature of the water, I figured she might not make it. So I told my boys to take in the sails as I darted below to start the engine. As the oldest boy sat on the mainsail to hold it down and the youngest son sat on the jib, my wife grabbed the life ring and I steered the boat for the woman who was already tiring and thrashing the water.

The men, who had no paddles and no way to get to her, had moments before refused our help. Now they were pleading and begging for us to hurry.

By the time we got to the woman, she was exhausted and struggling in the current to stay afloat. Thank God we were in time!

We had offered help earlier, but it was not until they all admitted they had a problem that we could do something to help them.

One of the keys to unlock your will and become a person of self-discipline is to admit you have a problem. Do not blame someone else for the problem. It is yours. It makes no sense to accuse your parents of a poor job of raising you, saying that is the reason you have no self-discipline.

If we invested the time striving to get control

of our lives that we spend complaining about life, we might be on our way to recovery.

After we admit we have the problem, we need to choose to do something about it. I call this driving a stake. When certain American Indians fought another tribe, the older warriors would sometimes drive a stake into the ground and lash one ankle to it. This meant that from this point I will not retreat. Right here I will live or die—I am lashed to the stake.

I want to challenge you to drive a stake that you are going to work on self-discipline. Admit you have a problem. Then write on a piece of paper, "Today I am going to start working on the need for self-discipline." Drive a stake on it.

Driving the stake does not guarantee success, but it says you are not going to quit trying.

A person who stays with a company for 30 years does so because he does not quit, even though he would like to.

People who celebrate their fiftieth wedding anniversary do so because they refused to quit.

There are times when I do well at disciplining myself and times when I am horrible at it, but I have learned not to quit.

IV

SELF-DISCIPLINE
AS A
SOURCE OF JOY

18

Self-Discipline and Our Talents

Your efforts at self-discipline may have been so unsatisfactory you cannot possibly consider self-discipline as a source of joy.

For us who struggle to bring our lives under control, our efforts at self-discipline have been some of our most frustrating times. We hear the word self-discipline and our mind is instantly negative. We have tried many times to bring self under control but the efforts have been more futile than satisfying.

Maybe I can help you look at things in a new light.

My wife is a musician. She holds her master's degree in percussion from the American Conservatory of Music in Chicago. Her instrument is the marimba. Mary's parents purchased her first instrument when she was 13 years old. Immediately she began taking lessons. In fact, she took lessons weekly through junior high, senior high, college, and graduate school.

She happened to live in Kansas City which at that time had an outstanding marimba teacher. There is no doubt in my mind she has profited from having good teachers. However, the lessons were not where my wife learned to play the marimba. That came when she practiced. And Mary practiced hard, before school and after school.

In fact she still practices today—more than 35 years later. Her instrument has been one of her great sources of joy.

During her high school years and after college she played in the Philharmonic Orchestra in Kansas City. She has travelled widely as a professional entertainer in her late teens and early 20's. After marriage, she travelled in many meetings with me. Today, with the children grown and gone, she is again venturing to concerts and tours.

I have noticed through the years that when she was unhappy or down she would turn to her instrument for solace and inspiration. She really enjoys playing the marimba. One reason is that she plays it so very well.

It has always been interesting to me that she

enjoys playing scales and exercises. She knows these are the disciplines that keep her in shape to perform in public.

The reason she receives so much joy from her music is she has paid a price in self-discipline which has allowed her a certain mastery of the marimba. Lessons were a part of her development and no doubt good instruction is a key for proper development in any area of skill. The heart of developing a gift or ability is practice.

In our travels we have met people who own marimbas and have them set up in their homes. In days past they may even have had lessons. But they do not play today because they did not exercise self-discipline in this area. So today my wife's instrument is a source of joy to her, while to others their marimba is treated like a piece of furniture. The difference is that Mary had a program of practice and worked at self-discipline to follow the program.

Frankly, it is no different in any area of life. Each of us has abilities which were given to us at birth. There are things all of us could do well if we would discipline ourselves and develop that talent and ability.

You may have an undeveloped organizational ability. Perhaps you enjoy people and have communication skills you have not fully developed. Writing may be a talent you have left dormant because writing is a work of self-discipline.

One thing I know from experience is that a person is happiest with himself when he is doing his best. When I played sports I always enjoyed winning. But I have had games when I was not pleased with my performance. Even though we won as a team, I was not happy about my performance. I have also lost games where I did my best and played my hardest. I did not enjoy losing but there was joy in knowing I had done my best and simply had been beaten by a better team.

My wife and I have a friend who is tremendously gifted musically. She is a singer-composer and has the talent to be someone truly outstanding. However, there is no self-discipline and, consequently, our friend always talks about what is going to happen. But things do not just happen unless you use self-discipline to maximize, develop, and use that gift and talent which is within you.

Every person has talents to be developed. The development and use of those talents is a source of joy. It is always thrilling to do your best. Self-discipline is the thing that makes the development of talents possible.

Self-discipline is a source of joy because it is the road we must travel to do our best.

19

Self-Discipline as a Time-Stretcher

During a recent morning broadcast the news department was showing some of the latest labor-saving devices available to the woman of the house to help her with food preparation and housework. When the interviewer asked the one representing these products why they had been developed, the answer came back, "We want to be able to give people more free time."

When the average person thinks of free time, he or she thinks of time for holidays or vacations. For some people, "free time" means time to pursue hobbies or to engage in your favorite physical activity, whether it be skiing, sailing, or skin diving.

I do have to admit that I have spent days

sailing, time away from work, that I could not really call free time. The reason it was not free is because my mind was not free. Things were left hanging. In my case, the sad part is that things were left undone not due to lack of time but due to lack of discipline on my part.

For time to be really free, necessary tasks need to be dealt with in a disciplined manner. Then when we go away to a free-time activity, it is really free time because mentally and emotionally we are free from the details of work.

Experience tells me that the person who is self-disciplined enjoys free time more and has more of it.

I can remember times when my wife, myself, and the boys would go to visit my mother. We would ask her to go with us to see someone or go out to eat or go for a ride. Most of the time she would reply that she did not have the time.

I have observed this in my own life. It is easy to feel that we have so many demands on us that we do not have any time for things we would like to do. Yet we see other people get their work done and make use of their free time for their own physical, mental, and emotional health, as well as that of their families.

Have you ever thought how you have the same number of hours in a day as they do? And some people do not have eight or nine days in their week and others only five—we all have seven.

Therefore, the key to making our free time free is to make our productive time *productive*. We lose free time when we waste productive time. In fact, waste enough productive time and when you take time to be free, you will find you are not free at all in your mind and spirit, but actually in *bondage* to what you left undone.

For a number of years I have taught people how to budget their money and how to stay on a budget. The initial response from people who think of budgeting for the first time is always the same: "I don't want to budget—I will be so confined in what I can spend."

People who have never budgeted before are startled to learn from experience that they do not have less money to do things they enjoy but more money because they do not waste it. They enjoy what they do even more fully because they have the funds to do it.

The nice thing about budgeting, which is really fiscal self-discipline, is when you learn to live within your income. When you get a raise, you can do even better.

Self-discipline in the management of time is even more important. There is no way to get a raise in time. By that I mean every hour has 60 minutes, every day 24 hours, and no matter how long we live, our days will not have more hours or our hours more minutes.

It therefore follows that the only way to find more free time is by making our productive time more productive. The way this is done is through exercising self-discipline both during periods of work and periods of play.

Then just as the budgeter learns he cannot create money by budgeting, he can make better use of what he has. The same is true with our productive time and our free time. Self-discipline is what makes it possible for us to enjoy them both.

For years I have lived my life by putting things off until the last minute, then cramming everything I need to do into a shortened time period. Thus I have many times done less than my best. Much of the time I have left things undone so when I did take off for a sail, a vacation, or a time away I was not really free. Rather, I was in bondage to the circumstances created by my lack of self-discipline.

Maybe this sounds familiar—even too familiar —to you. If it does, join me in saying, "I may not be able to control everything in my life every day, but by God's grace and with His help I am going to control one thing today and then reward myself with some free time which will *really* be free time."

20

Self-Discipline: Rewards That Last

There is a saying abroad in our land today, "I'm going to do my own thing."

When workaholic parents are asked about their neglect of the family, especially the children, you hear the reply: "Every person needs to do what they think is right and I'm going to do my own thing."

When the wayward child is questioned about a life-style that may include drinking, drugs, and inactivity—a life without purpose—the reply is, "Get off my back! I want to do my own thing."

We see people everywhere who are challenging authority. It may be parental, school, the boss' authority, or even legal authority. They justify their actions with, "Well, I've got my rights, too, you know—I just want to do my own thing."

We should not be surprised by this as we live in a world that has lost its God-consciousness. Our children are now taught that the *theory* of evolution is a fact—they are not on earth as a result of God's creative act. People no longer learn they are unique in all the universe, for out of all God's creation, they alone are made in His image. As man, they were created to be His friends, responsible and responsive.

Our children and grandchildren grow up thinking they are highly evolved animals who can act and react as animals do, giving vent to needs and concerns in any way they choose.

Is it any wonder we see people struggling to control themselves when advertisers tell us the good life consists of things, places, and pleasures rather than quality, character, and honesty? We are told we only go around once so we need to go for the gusto—and we believe it. The truth is, we do only go around once, but we need to get control of our lives so we can make the *most* of this one trip, not throw ourselves away on gusto.

A television commercial plugs a credit card to solve the tedium in our life. It will fill our rooms with things, our time with travel, and satisfy our appetites for exotic and erotic living. We are led to believe we can have it all *now*, but we are not told about the bondage that follows when the bills start to arrive. After all, what good does it do to tell people what they sow they will reap? They are sure the route to happiness and joy is to "do it my way."

What future is there for a voice like mine that calls people to become accountable for their actions? I feel like a voice crying in the wilderness saying life is best lived as a qualitative accomplishment, not a quantitative experience. What chance do I have calling a generation to self-discipline rather than self-indulgence?

One of the most popular singing voices of all time carries a message opposite to mine. His signature song says, "I'll do it my way." My voice calls out for self-control for God and man, to hundreds. His voice rings in the ears of millions and declares himself to be the master of his own fate.

My message is timely and timeless but easily forgotten. His message is clothed in a tune that stirs our emotions and captures our mind as we turn off the radio still humming, "I'll do it my way."

The biggest thing in favor of my message is it produces qualities that *last*, not experiences that fade.

Hear these words of a famous religious statesman:

In a race, everyone runs but only one person gets first prize. So run your race to win. To win the contest you must deny yourselves many things that would keep you from doing your best. An athlete goes to all this trouble just to win a blue ribbon or a silver cup, but we do it for a heavenly reward that never disappears. So I run straight to the goal with purpose in every step. I fight to win. I'm not shadow-boxing or playing around. Like an athlete I punish my body, treating it roughly, training it to do what it should, not what it wants to. Otherwise I fear that after enlisting others for the race, I myself might be declared unfit and ordered to stand aside (1 Corinthians 9:24-27).

In my heart I am attempting to draw a line. On one side is the call to follow the voice of this age which says, "I'll do it my way." On the other side is the ageless voice which calls, "Like an athlete, punish your body, treat it roughly, training it to do what it should, not what it wants to do."

21

Self-Discipline Versus Self-Indulgence

I spoke recently with the owner of a sizable corporation employing about 1,500 people. We were talking about hiring workers, particularly executives and managers. He confirmed again what other business leaders have said to me. The most frequently asked questions by the person being interviewed for a job are: "What are the benefits? What about vacations? When do I get my first one and what are the retirement benefits?"

Before working one day—before even being hired, college graduates as well as laborers are more interested in how they are going to be advantaged with time to indulge themselves than they are in ways to help the company and its opportunities for the future.

"You owe it to yourself" is the sales pitch of the retailers and advertising people. People using credit cards are building a strong wall of debt about themselves. The debtor's prison, a place you were thrown when you could not pay your debts is supposed to be a thing of the past. However, individuals are building their own personal prisons out of plastic credit cards and the debts they create.

It is all so easy. We are brainwashed to believe we owe it to ourselves to go, buy, eat, wear — and pay for it all later. Americans are spending money to keep up with people who do not care.

On television we see people smiling and rushing out with their family to spend money eating. In the background a full orchestra and choir perform in stereo the catchy ditty, "You deserve a break today, so get up and get away." For what? A hamburger!

Let's turn a page in the manual of self-indulgence and look at it from another perspective.

Procrastination is a form of self-indulgence. When you are choosing to put something off, you are indulging yourself. For any number of reasons we might judge this task to be too hard, too long, beneath us — or we may be afraid of failure, or even afraid of success, so we put it off. If we do that, we have indulged ourselves.

Many people seem to think the path of happiness is self-indulgence. Don't believe it for a moment. The drug addict who dies of an overdose keeps indulging himself until he overloads his system. The person who becomes angry and murders someone has just indulged himself in bitterness, hate, and violence.

The person who is forever pressing someone for sexual relationships is guilty of self-indulgence. We have been led to believe self-indulgence is the path of happiness and fun. The person who denies himself some of the above activities is looked upon as old-fashioned.

Something degrading is being said about our society when we precede the words honesty, integrity, commitment, and self-discipline with "old-fashioned."

Our nation is in a financial struggle today. Everyone is aware that we must begin cutbacks in government spending and programs to get the national debt turned around. But when we start thinking of what to cut, each of us wants to cut the other guy's program. Why? Because we are a self-indulgent society. "Take his, but don't touch mine" is our feeling.

In my opinion our nation is not in a deficit crisis; our people are in a self-discipline crisis. Listen to Solomon's words from Proverbs:

Listen to me, my son! I know what I am saying; listen! Watch yourself, lest you be indiscreet and betray some vital information . . . lest strangers obtain your wealth, and you become a slave to foreigners . . . and you say, "Oh, if only I had listened! If only I had not demanded my own way" (Proverbs 5:1, 2,10,12).

In counseling people I have heard them use these words often: "Oh, if only I had listened; if only I had not demanded my own way."

I know relationships in business that have been severed by self-indulgence and saved by self-discipline.

I know fortunes that have been lost through self-indulgence and others that have been won through self-discipline.

I know homes that have split up through self-indulgence and homes that have been strengthened through self-discipline.

Let's quit fooling ourselves; we are not self-indulgent because others cause us to be. We are self-indulgent because we choose the easy way—we yield to the spirit of the age.

Self-discipline, not self-indulgence, is the road to happiness and joy.

V

MAINTAINING
SELF-DISCIPLINE

22

Plan Periods of Rest

One of the great joys of self-discipline is that it gives you more time to do something besides work. Some people think about self-discipline and making the most of their time and get all hung up thinking there will be no free time for their pursuit of personal enjoyment. Just the opposite is true. When you make good use of your time taking care of work activities, your free time is really *free*.

We not only have to have a block of time which we do not owe to some other activity, but we must have completed our work so our mind is free. Thus we are ready to enter into some pleasurable pursuit and give our mind, emotion, and energy to this time of enjoyment.

There is a neglected but important passage in Mark 6:30,31:

> The apostles now returned to Jesus from their tour and told him all they had done and what they had said to the people they visited. Then Jesus suggested, "Let's get away from the crowds for a while and rest." For so many people were coming and going that they scarcely had time to eat.

One of my favorite Baptist preachers, Vance Havner, says, "We all need to come apart to rest before we come apart, period."

You and I need to understand the importance of rest and relaxation. Our nervous sytem is like a well. You can hook a pump to a well and pump and pump it. As long as there is rain and snow to replace the water table in the well you can keep on pumping and the water will be clean and good.

But when there is a drought and the water table is lowered, you can pump that well until it goes dry. When you get near the bottom the water is brackish, smelly, cloudy, and will not be enjoyed. When this happens there is nothing you can do until the refreshing rains come and the water table is raised.

It is possible to become so involved in activity,

so self-disciplined to work only, that you can pump the nervous system dry and break down. Sometimes people say they are burned out on some job.

When that happens their disposition becomes brackish as their emotions are drained and they may find themselves more discouraged than they have ever been. Then the normally positive person will become a negative influence or may break down and weep for no apparent reason. Depression is often part of the profile of those who pump their nervous and emotional systems dry.

The difficult thing to achieve in life is proper balance. Poverty and spirituality are not synonymous. But at the same time we can be so materialistic and thing-oriented that we lose sight of the eternal.

One of my wife's criticisms of me, which is totally valid, is I have a hard time doing things in moderation. With me a thing is all work—work all the time—or a total abandonment of work and an all-out commitment to pleasure.

Consequently, both myself and my family have missed some times that could have been delightful. My ability to stop and smell the flowers daily has not been good. So I will commit to some large-scale sailing trip and find myself working so hard at it that I turn this experience into an all-out effort causing the activity to be devoid of simple, old-fashioned fun.

You and I both know people who have spent all their time in activities to help kids while their own children fell apart without them noticing until it was too late. *Balance is the key.*

Put on your schedule times when you will not work. Block out days for travel. Everyone needs at least three things he enjoys doing with his hands and needs to be wise enough to schedule time to do them. My three things are model shipbuilding, woodworking, and embroidery. I chose embroidery because it makes nice gifts, plus it is an easy hobby to take with me when I travel.

I know only one way to achieve balance in the self-discipline of work and rest. Just as you have been challenged to plan to get control of your life, so you must plan to rest.

23

Plan Around Pressure Periods

To begin a life of self-control, we need to predetermine our difficult pressure periods and plan around them.

If you are dealing with a self-discipline problem of productivity in your office, think about what keeps you from it. Have you fallen into a habit of starting your day with chatter in the hall or the early-morning coffee treat as you begin the day? I have watched people fall into such a repetitious pattern that they meet the same people in the same place at the same time nearly every day and chat away 15 or 20 minutes of time. If this describes you, perhaps you need to change your habit patterns. Try entering the building through a different door. Leave home ten minutes earlier so you miss the chatter.

If you have set as your exercise time a 6 A.M. visit to the club on the way to work for a one-hour workout, then a healthy breakfast and into the office before 8 A.M., you must have a plan to deal with what might interrupt that.

The classic interruption is when you have been gone for three days and your flight is delayed and instead of arriving at 9:00, it gets in at 11:30. You had hoped to be in bed by 10:30, but you finally fall in bed exhausted at 1 A.M.

When the alarm goes off at 5:30 and you have not had enough sleep to have a good exercise period, what do you do? On the way home on the flight you knew you were going to have this problem. That was the time to solve the problem with predetermined action, not at 5:30 in the morning.

My suggestion is get up, go to the club, do very little exercise, sit in the sauna or hot tub, but do your best to keep your continuity. Do not wake up after four-and-a-half hours of sleep and tell yourself how sleepy you are, what a hard trip it was, and then go back to sleep promising yourself you will work out after work. Chances are, with that approach, you will feel doubly guilty. You will feel guilty for going back to sleep. Next, you will probably not meet your appointment with yourself to exercise after work.

On your trip you went through two time zones.

You are struggling with jet lag and by the time work is over, you feel less like exercising than you did when you started. So you have just programmed yourself to fail and you are going to feel guilty at night also. If you feel guilty enough and have a bad day at work, it is easy to convince yourself that self-discipline is possible for others but not for you, and you find it easy to abandon the whole exercise program.

If this scenario sounds vaguely familiar, then realize we all go through these battles. The way to victory is to have decided *ahead* what you are going to do when the problem shows itself.

An area of self-discipline I struggle with daily is my eating and my weight. For years I have used three great cop-outs as to why I was overweight. One was that I travel a lot and eat in restaurants most of the time. My second one was I work hard, go on five to six hours sleep, so I need fuel to keep the fire burning as my schedule takes a lot of energy. The third cop-out made about as much sense as the first two. I am with people in their homes and the entertaining they do is too much for me to resist.

Now there is an element of truth in each of these. I do eat in restaurants a lot, I do function on a few hours of sleep, and I am entertained in many nice homes.

The answer to my eating and weight problem is simple if I set my predetermined plan in motion.

I seldom read the menu for breakfast or lunch in a restaurant. I simply order a poached egg or fresh fruit and do not even start thinking about strawberry waffles or eggs Benedict. If due to my schedule I need nourishment or a snack, I reach for fresh fruit instead of a piece of pie. I can also eat in the finest homes if I simply take a modest portion of everything and no seconds.

Nothing will relieve the stress and ensure the success of your plans as well as having a predetermined plan to carry you through those inevitable pressure periods.

24

Call Yourself to Accountability

One thing I did at age 40 was to make a written statement of the purpose of my life. I have long since memorized it and it is now a part of my empirical data bank that affects my attitude and actions.

The purpose of my life is to know God through His Son Jesus, to live empowered by the Holy Spirit, and to have my life under control so I can wed my ability to God's opportunity and use what comes out of that union for His honor and glory. God is not honored by a believer's life being out of control.

In an effort to get my life under I have developed a principle of "calling myself to constant accountability." Here is how it works. I work each day out of a date book system. There are two pages for each day. On the left page is a place for appointments—things to do and expenses. On the right page is a place to keep a diary of what I do. When I work, I keep the date book beside me and write down each thing I do in the time slot I do it. This means that each day I know who called me, whom I called, what memos and letters I wrote, and the projects I worked on. I have often been known to say I can tell you when I was in the airport in Chicago, what time I put twenty-five cents in the phone, whom I called, and what we talked about.

This is not an easy thing for me. It has gotten easier as the years roll by. There are lapses in my system, periods when I have difficult schedules and bad days. But this is my system. This is what I work at—calling myself to constant accountability.

The reason for this is simple. I have a very difficult time with self-discipline. From experience I have learned I can get to the end of a day and have accomplished nothing or very little. Put five of those together and you have a wasted week. I have done that many times and get more depressed as each wasted day goes by.

So I developed the principle of committing myself to constant accountability.

You can do the same as I do or you may prefer a modified form. Instead of keeping a daily diary of all you do, you could keep a record of what you have chosen to work on in your program of self-discipline. For example, if you seek a disciplined program of exercise, you could begin to keep a log of your activities.

I know of two associate pastors who play racquetball three times per week. This is a commitment made to themselves and to each other. Each has a home computer and keeps track of all his scores so they can run averages for a week, month, or year and thus keep themselves working hard at trying to improve. By carefully monitoring what they do, they are always striving to improve.

Using this system sounds like drudgery, but I find the opposite to be true. It is wonderfully satisfying to finish a day and be able to look back over my book and see what is completed.

I have often thought the hourly wage system might be a curse. Too many people are concerned with how many hours they have put in, instead of what they have accomplished.

Another thing I like about calling myself to constant accountability is that it keeps me focused on what I should be doing. It is no joy to write down things that you know are a waste of time.

Victor Hugo wrote, "When the disposal of time is surrendered to the chance of incidents, chaos will reign." No truer statement could be made of some periods in my life. At times I have let phone calls, drop-ins, long-lost friends, the mail, or a catalog sidetrack me.

When I follow the principle of calling myself to constant accountability, I find I can concentrate intently. How many times have we gone to a meeting where a problem has been discussed for 30 minutes or more and when the meeting breaks up, there is no specific understanding of who does what and when? This does not happen if you are calling yourself to constant accountability.

When I keep track of what I do as I do it, I find myself far more willing to follow the plan I have set in motion for that particular day. Focus is so important in self-discipline. It helps you spend your time on what counts.

25

Keep Trying!

Another key to self-discipline is to accept the fact that you will have to start again many times.

I admire the way my wife, Mary, has the ability to set a program in motion, have it interrupted, and simply start over again. For example, she has herself on an exercise program to do aerobics with the television at 9 A.M. and then go ride her bicycle. I have seen her do this for four days in a row or for two weeks daily. Then her schedule will be interrupted by travel or by my coming home from a trip. She will not be able to keep her schedule for a day or two. Upon returning home she can go immediately back to her program as if she never missed a day.

I have always had a problem doing that. I can set an exercise time and start in and carry on daily. But have something interrupt it, and I will abandon the whole thing rather than return to it.

I have a fear of failure when I set such a program in motion. It is enough of a problem to me that this mental lapse has kept me from starting some things that I should be doing.

Slowly, I am learning that we all struggle to control ourselves and there is no perfect plan for performance. It has helped me deal with the problem by simply recognizing I have the problem and realizing I can never keep any program perfectly that I set up. When there are lapses in the discipline (and there will be), I simply accept that as a fact of life and get back on track as I have opportunity to do so.

There is a part of my self-image problem that makes it very easy for me to quit. For my wife quitting is a hard thing—for me it is an easy thing.

One lesson I keep learning and forgetting and learning again is that we all have problems and at times we want to quit.

I remember when David, my oldest son, was about 9 and wanted to take piano lessons. We talked about it and I told him he could on two conditions. One, he had to agree to practice. I knew that his mother, who loves to practice her music, would do her best to see he practiced, but I wanted him to agree to practice.

The second condition was that he would begin when school started and would take lessons until school was out. If during the year he did not like the piano, it did not matter. He was to take lessons until school was out in June and then we would decide at that time if he wanted to continue.

You can probably guess what happened. About January he informed me he did not like the piano and he was going to quit. As best I could, I attempted to show him there were many things and many times I wanted to quit too. Then I dropped the bomb—he had to hold to the agreement and finish the year.

"At times we all want to quit," I told him, "but we don't quit." I said, "Dave, I am going to give you permission to talk about quitting all you want. Your frustration level may be such you will need to verbalize that you want to quit. That is going to be okay as long as you understand you won't quit until the agreement is up."

Knowing my own tendency to quit, I have attempted to encourage my sons in a more aggressive pursuit to complete tasks.

There is a difference between wanting to quit and quitting. It has been a help to me to realize wanting to quit is natural. At times we have all felt like we wanted to quit. Learning self-discipline will test you sorely on this point. There are times you will not be able to stay on the program you set up. From time to time you will feel like you are spinning your wheels. You will want to quit. Accept that as a fact, but decide that you are not going to quit.

Verbalize that you want to quit as long as you understand you *will not* quit. Your program may have been interrupted and you are frustrated. Pick one thing to do, a time to do it, and get back on track. Keep trying. You will be amazed at how you can take control of your life if you simply keep trying.

26

Make Solitude and Prayer a Priority

Martin Luther was heard to remark, "I have so many things to do tomorrow I must get up early to spend an extra hour in prayer and meditation."

For too long, people have thought just the opposite. Too many times my attitude is that I have so much to do tomorrow that I am sure God will forgive me if I do not get alone with Him for meditation and prayer.

There is a beautiful verse in Mark 1:35:

"The next moment he [speaking of Jesus] was up long before daybreak and went out alone into the wilderness to pray."

Good things take place when we spend time

121

alone with God. Cleansing takes place, faith grows, our purpose grows, life is more vigorous, and our enthusiasm is up. There are so many good things we find built in our lives when we get alone with God.

Solitude and prayer are interesting concepts. They give us courage and strength. Think for a moment about the life of our Lord Jesus. Before every major crisis in His life, He got alone with God.

Before the temptation by the devil prior to the opening of His ministry, Jesus spent 40 days in prayer and fasting. The night before He called the 12 disciples, He spent the night in prayer.

Where was He when they came to arrest and take Him to trial and eventually crucify Him? He was in Gethsemane in a garden, praying.

The disciples recognized that not only was prayer important to Jesus, but it was important for them. In Luke 11:1, the disciples asked for help:

> Once when Jesus had been out praying, one of his disciples came to him as he finished and said, "Lord, teach us a prayer to recite just as John taught one to his disciples."

Jesus responded with an illustration:

> Suppose you went to a friend's house at midnight, wanting to borrow three loaves of bread. You would shout up to him, "A friend

of mine has just arrived for a visit and I've nothing to give him to eat." He would call down from his bedroom, "Please don't ask me to get up. The door is locked for the night and we are all in bed. I just can't help you this time." But I'll tell you this—though he won't do it as a friend, if you keep on knocking long enough he will get up and give you everything you want—just because of your persistence. And so it is with prayer. Keep on asking and you will keep on getting; keep on looking and you will keep on finding; knock and the door will be opened (Luke 11:5-9).

Here are words from our Lord Jesus that carry power and promise. But few people allow these words to affect their lives. I believe there is a strength that comes to people who are able to spend some time alone with God.

For people to have strength of character, they must be committed to a well-thought-out value system. In business there is no such thing as being a little dishonest. One is either honest or dishonest. If you lose your moral integrity, you may do well for a while but you will be exposed. Eventually you will be the loser.

A well-thought-out value system does not just happen. People who hold to principles have spent time thinking them through.

One of my big concerns about our nation is that too many of our people seem to be afraid to be alone. How many times have you gone into a home and the television will be on but nobody will be watching it? On airplanes I see people with their personal stereos banging away at their ears. I am concerned we are losing the strength one gets from being alone, thinking things through, and then committing yourself to a principle.

Form the good habit of spending some time alone each day in prayer and meditation. Many times I find I go from such an experience directly into a planning session of what I want to get done and how to do it.

In order to seek solitude, you need to set a time to do it; have a place to go to; and have a Bible, prayer list, and materials ready for use.

All areas of self-discipline become easier when you have gathered courage, strength, and vigor during your solitude.

This might be the key you have needed. If you have struggled with self-control or self-discipline, get out your paper and pencil and choose to start with a daily time of solitude. Write down on the paper *when* you will do it, *where* you will do it, and *what* you will do when you get there. As you find strength in your solitude, you will find new resolve to deal with other areas of your life.

If our Lord felt the need to get alone with the Father, then this ought to be a priority for us.

27

Learn to Love the Process

Therefore if any man is in Christ, he
is a new creature; old things passed
away; behold, new things have come
(2 Corinthians 5:17 NASB).

When on September 23, 1953, I placed saving
faith in Jesus Christ, I became a new creature.
From the moment I received Christ, my life
became a transformed experience. My language
changed, my desires changed, my priorities were
rearranged.

The struggle since that night has been to exercise self-discipline and live out the Christian life.
Paul speaks of this struggle in Philippians
2:12,13:

So then, my beloved, just as you have always obeyed, not as in my presence only, but now much more in my absence, work out your salvation with fear and trembling; for it is God who is at work in you, both to will and to work for His good pleasure (NASB).

Part of what Paul is telling the church at Philippi is that living out the Christian life is an ongoing process of change through self-discipline. Living the Christian life is dealing with problems every day, facing and answering them from a Christian perspective.

In America Christians have difficulty dealing with the problems of the Christian life on a daily basis. In our culture we are accustomed to having problems dealt with in an instant.

Sports are a big part of people's lives in this country. Could one of the reasons why the American public is so enamored with sports be that there is a contest of will, strength, and agility which begins and ends in two or three hours? When you watch a sports event, whether your team wins or loses the contest is over in a short time.

Life is not like that. Life continues day after day. I remember crossing the campus of Seattle Pacific University and meeting one of my professors. In greeting him I said, "Good morning,

Doctor. How's life?" As he passed me his reply was simple. "Everyday" was all he said. So it is. Life is a daily experience.

Believers seem to want the life they see in the average TV production. In one hour the worst possible situations will be created and then solved. People have come to expect the same thing in their lives.

When there is a problem in their marriage, they want a book, a promise, or a prayer that is going to solve the problem right now. We have become a people of the immediate.

In his message to the Philippians, Paul is telling them that changing is a process. Physical birth happens following months of pregnancy. Once a person is born there is a life to be lived. Spiritual rebirth takes place following years of the germination of the seed of the Word of God. Once the rebirth takes place, there is a spiritual life to be lived out in a physical body among people who must live within the parameters of the curse of God upon sin.

May God help us to understand that change is a lifelong process. There is no one thing we can do to bring an instant solution to many of life's problems. We must choose self-discipline and learn to love the ongoing, day-to-day process of change.